Table of Contents

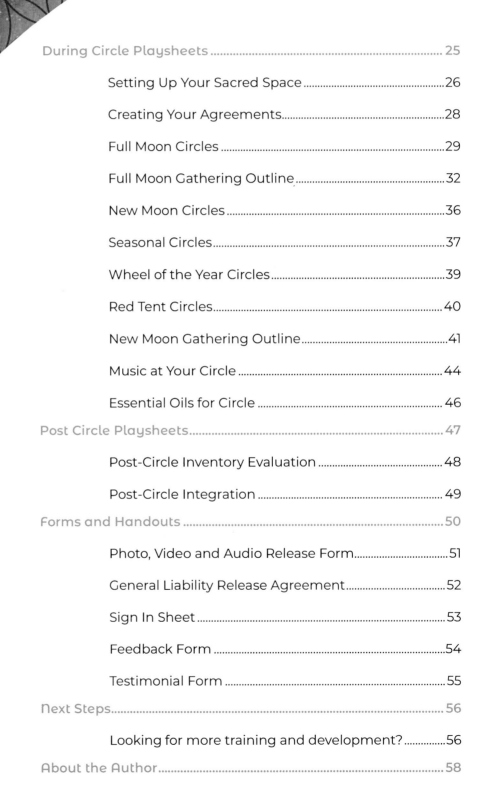

The Art of Leading Circle

– Startup Kit –

Pre Circle Playsheets

How to Start Your First Circle

*L*ike most things, getting started is the hardest part. It takes courage, perseverance, faith and determination to start anything. It's what distinguishes someone as successful.

Napoleon Hill shares a story about a miner who was digging straight down in the earth and quit while the gold jackpot was three feet away to the side of where he was digging. The next guy comes in, digs at a diagonal and hits the vein, striking gold.

This analogy is exactly why most businesses fail, most people struggle to be entrepreneurs and, in our case, most circles don't get started.

So the question is, how do you actually get that first circle started? Because once you do the first one, you know you can do it again.

First, we want to distinguish what gets in the way of starting a circle, then dive into the easiest strategy to get started.

What holds you back

I've interviewed hundreds of women who want to start a circle, asking them what holds them back. And it comes down to one core belief: *the fear of not being good enough*. There are 4 ways this shows up:

- ꙮ Fear that no one will show up
- ꙮ Fear of letting down those who show up by not fulfilling their expectations so they won't come back
- ꙮ Fear of not being taken seriously
- ꙮ Fear of someone hijacking the circle and not being able to effectively manage it

If you can identify with any of these fears, there is good news: you are not alone. And even better news: it's not actually *real*.

You are making these things up! Why do I say this: because you are making assumptions based on something that has not happened yet and if it is your first time, there is no actual evidence that this will happen!

It's based on your past … all the times you took action and tasted some flavor of "failure."

So you have a choice: you can either be stopped by the fear, or take a lesson from it and take a new action that will produce a different result.

If you knew that there was a proven system that worked, you would feel more confident, right? And if you took these actions step by step, you would believe that things may be different, right?

That's where I come in: *to give you the proven action plan and activate your feminine leadership so you take the inspired, imperfect action.*

The only caveat is that you have to believe in Sistership Circle, yourself, a higher power, and sisterhood. You don't even need to believe in me (because ultimately, your back-door may be: well, it works for some people but not me).

(Our programs helps you to overcome the fears and step into *believing*.)

If you are ready to let go of the fear and step into believing, then read on.

Step 1: Clarify
Know Your Why

*W*hen we start a circle, we need to work on both our inner and outer game. Our inner game is our belief system and inner strength. It's who we are being, which is based on what we are thinking and feeling. Our outer game is the actions we take based on the plan and strategy. There are four tenets to make up a supportive belief system and build our core, inner strength:

Courage - this is the strength needed to take action despite the fear

Trust - allowing others to contribute to you (including spirit)

Faith - letting go of control and allowing spirit to guide us

Perseverance - never giving up mentally (faith) and physically (action)

These four tenets are rooted in a solid foundation, which is your WHY. The more connected you are with your personal WHY, the easier it is to have courage, trust, faith and perseverance.

While we are taught that focusing on yourself is selfish and we should be selfless to lead circle, I find the opposite to be true. When I focus on what I want to get out of it and what benefits I will receive from circle, I then open up the space for others to give themselves permission to claim their desires, too.

Why do you want a circle FOR YOU? Put aside leading and helping others. How will this help YOU?

_____

_____

_____

_____

Why is sisterhood important to you? What happened in your past? What pain have you suffered? How bad was it? Get to the core desire and need. Did your mother abandon you? Did your best friend turn against you? Did you get bullied? Who hurt your feelings? Did you have a tipping point?

_____

_____

_____

_____

_____

_____

The more you feel this, the stronger your why. How urgent is this? Find the urgency at a level 10. _If you are struggling because it feels like a blindspot, I am available for power coaching to activate this within you. Email_ tanya@sistershipcircle.com _with the subject line POWER COACHING SESSION REQUEST and tell me a little about what you are looking for support in._

_____

_____

_____

_____

Once you connect with your story that gets to your WHY, you are primed for a powerful circle. Your WHY will energetically attract other women who share that same WHY. Like attracts like. This is an important distinction.

Step 2: Envision

Set Your Intention

The next piece is to set your intention. What do you want to call in? What will the circle provide you? (again, don't worry about what it will provide the women ... they will get what they are supposed to get)

_____

_____

_____

_____

What will be possible from being in circle? What will you experience? How will it feel? Write whatever comes to you.

_____

_____

_____

_____

🎧 **Listen to my audio visualization to call in your circle: https://s3.amazonaws.com/ stream-tribal/Facilitator+Tribe/Meditations/Visualization_+Creating+Your+Circle.m4a.**

My Path To Getting Started

In January 2009, I put on my first event. It wasn't a circle, but a speaker event where 30 women showed up. I was new to the area so I knew only a couple women from my past, the rest I had been introduced to, or had come because a friend recommended it. I then did monthly gatherings for a year before I put on a Launch Event in January 2010. I continued to do monthly events until I started the first 12-week program in June 2010.

I share my path to show you that a) I had no idea what I was doing, I just did it and b) you need to just get started. It doesn't matter who shows up. It doesn't matter if you know anyone. It doesn't matter if you've facilitated before.

Inspired action (based on your WHY) == >> Confidence == >> More inspired action

(it's cyclical)

The Sistership Circle Path

Here at Sistership Circle, we have a full business model that includes monthly gatherings, 8-12 week circle programs, retreats and 1:1 coaching with the Feminine Freedom Method.

We recommend that you lead at least 6 monthly gatherings before offering a circle program.

If you are ambitious and have a successful first circle with 20+ women, we recommend putting on a big splash (that is the most time and resource leveraged) Launch Party.

Choose your level

Level A: a small gathering in your living room (6 women)

Level B: a mid-sized event (20 women) at a local space or very nice house

Level C: Launch event (40+ women)

Assessment

- ○ Do you have a large network?
- ○ Do you have an email list?
- ○ Do you go to networking events?
- ○ Are you social?
- ○ Is it easy for you to make invitations?

- ○ Have you hosted a party, event or gathering before?
- ○ Are you a Type A Personality?
- ○ Are you a natural leader?

If you answered Yes to 1-3 out of 8, then I recommend Level A. If you answered 4-6 out of 8, then I recommend Level B. If you answered 6+, then I recommend you choose between B and C.

Step 3: Commit

Set Your Date & Venue

Declare a Date

Before commitment, there is hesitation and the chance to draw back. Once you commit, all of the universe moves to conspire with you to manifest your intention.

To commit, all you need to do is set a date. It's that simple! Pick a date that works for you.

_____

_____

_____

FAQ:

What day of the week should I host circle on?

Really, it's up to you. Which day do you prefer? Go with that. There will always be women who can't make it. Stand in your desire and you'll attract the right women. When you start trying to please others, you'll attract more difficulty.

I prefer Monday evening for a regular circle and Thursday evening for a gathering.

Evening or daytime?

Again, depends on your preference. Usually, everyone can make it in the evening. You could do 6 - 9pm on a weekday. Or an early morning circle 8 - 10am. Or a brunch on a weekend 10 - 1pm.

What time?

Again, what do you prefer?

We like to do potluck 6:30 - 7pm and circle 7 - 9 pm.

To potluck or not to potluck?

The benefit of potluck is that everyone gets to connect on a more chatty level before they drop into deeper circle space. They also get to arrive on time and get something to eat.

However, it may not be conducive to the venue. If you decide not to do potluck, ask women to arrive 15 minute before your intended start time so that you have everyone in the room ready to go on time.

Also, I highly recommend discouraging alcohol from being served. It can create an unsafe environment for those who are not drinking.

How much time should I give myself for promotion?

Usually we start to promote our circles 2-4 weeks in advance. I would say 3 weeks is a good standard amount of promotion time. Remember, the majority doesn't register for an event until the week of (and usually the day before).

If people RSVP on a Facebook event, make sure you give them reminders because they will tend to forget. Asking for a formal RSVP or registration on a website is always best to get commitment.

Finding a Venue

I prefer to host circle in a home ... and especially my home to make it convenient for me. My living room is small (roughly 13x16ft), but if we move all the furniture, can squeeze 15-20 women on the floor in a circle.

If you feel blocked in this area, know that this is NOT the most important thing. First, identify the block. Is it that you don't want to pay for a venue? Don't know where to go? Never had to deal with a venue before? Whatever the block is, it is actually making it more difficult for the perfect venue to show up.

Surrender the venue to the universe.
As woo-woo as it sounds, it works. The perfect venue will come to you effortlessly as soon as you let go of your attachment to it and the belief that it's hard to find.

"I surrender to you, Goddess. Please send me the perfect venue for my gathering where women will feel peaceful, connected and alive in their feminine."

Put it out there.
Start asking friends and put a post on Facebook asking for recommendations. Someone's bound to have an idea that resonates with you.

Research local venues.

Yoga studios. Coffee Shops. Wellness centers. Schools. Libraries. In the summer: a local park or a bonfire at the beach. All are potentials.

Ask a sister to host at her home.

Do you have a friend who has a gorgeous living room space? Ask if she'll host for you in exchange for something. Some people LOVE to be the hostess and would graciously say YES!

FAQ:

Which is better - a free venue or a paid venue?

It depends. I personally prefer a free venue hosted at a woman's home because it creates the atmosphere that I am looking for: comfortable, safe and homey. The goddess of circles is Hestia, who is the goddess of the hearth. Having circle in front of a fireplace makes it cozy and nurturing.

If you need to find a paid venue, then I suggest charging for the event either as an upfront fee or donation based. If you do donation, then at the end of the event, calculate how many women there are and how much the venue cost and then let the women know it is $x per person to cover the cost of the venue.

Here are some suggestions for negotiating with a space:

To avoid risk, do a revenue share of 70 (you) - 30 (venue) or less for the venue

1) In general the cost of a venue should be no more than $90 for a 3-hour event (unless you are renting a larger space that holds 100+ people).

2) Create some exchange. Perhaps the venue gets free admission for their guests in exchange for a free venue. Or if they have a cafe, people can purchase food/drink before the circle.

I think I want to do my circle outside. What's the pros and cons between indoor or outdoor circles?

An outdoor circle is great during the summer, especially if you are doing a fire ceremony. Make sure you have lights and tell women to bring blankets and pillows. If it is during the day, make sure you have a shade structure and tell women to wear a hat and sunscreen.

The cons of an outdoor circle: unpredictable weather, distractions from other people if in a public space, harder to hold the container, and lighting if at night.

I prefer indoor circles no matter what the time of year because the walls of the room help me hold the container and I don't have to worry about noise, weather or lighting.

Step 4: Share

Put The Word Out There!

*Y*ou've got a date, now announce it to your world. Whoever is in your world who is interested will naturally be attracted to it and say yes.

Best Practices

Here are my suggested tips to find women in the following order of priority:

Personal Invites

The #1 way to have women show up for your circle is to make sincere and heartfelt personal invitations. It's as if you are inviting your best girlfriends over for an intimate conversation. Share who this woman is for you, why you want her to be there, and what she will get out of it.

It can be on the phone, in person, via text, on Facebook messenger or an email.

For example:

> *Sue, you are one of my favorite friends because you have such a big heart and always show up for me. I'm hosting my first women's circle where we will be discussing Self-Love and I'd love for you to be there, not only because your support would help me feel more confident in leading, but also because I think you will walk away feeling filled up, nourished and supported. Can you make it on Sept 30?*

Social Media

Always create a Facebook event for your circle and share about it on your social media networks. There is a little thing called Social Proofing that you should know about.

Social credibility and proofing happens when I post an event on Facebook, and a woman clicks that she is attending, it shows up in her Facebook feed. When her friends see it and are curious, they click to see what it is. The more that people say yes, the more people see it. This is organic traffic.

Now if you add in asking your friends to share it, you have it working double time for you! Facebook has an algorithm that favors popular posts and events. The more likes, the more people attending, the more comments, the higher Facebook ranks it in the newsfeed.

At this point, all you need to do is create an event, invite people, share it on your newsfeed, and let it do its thing. If you want, you can ask your friends who have said they are coming to also share it, but this isn't required.

Ask friends to bring friends

Imagine if you invited 3 friends and asked each of them to bring 3 friends. You then have 9 women at your circle! You don't have to do this alone. The more you can ask for help from your friends, the easier this will be.

Networking

There are so many networking events these days that you can go to and share about your circle. If someone says, "What do you do?" You respond: "I help women connect with one another at my women's circles." If she asks for more info, invite her to attend!

Networking doesn't have to be at an official event. Set an intention that every time you leave your house, you will meet a woman who is interested in your circle. If you run into someone you know, and she asks "What's new?" then invite her.

Hubs

Hubs are women who are natural leaders and are the life of the party. Do you know any women who are the networkers, host events themselves, or are good at bringing people together?

Connect with these women and invite them to your circle. Frame it as "what's in it for her." Perhaps she can lead the opening meditation for the circle. When you ask women to contribute in a collaborative way, they want to show up.

Connecting and collaborating with other leaders has been the #1 source to building my circles.

Meetup.com

I'm a little wary of Meetup.com because a lot of people say they are going to events and then don't show up. It's a great way to get the word out, but offer women an incentive to actually attend. Or reach out to them personally and make a connection before the circle so they feel more of a pull toward committing.

Flyers

I have never connected with making flyers and leaving them places because they don't have the social proofing that social media has, but if you want to do this, go for it. We have templates for our members to use. I suggest making sure you have a testimonial on there and an inviting photo to draw women in.

Who to invite?

Sit in meditation and see who comes to mind. These women are your first women to invite and let them know that. Make an invitation from the heart.

Be open to who the Goddess wants to be there. Really, it's not totally up to you who comes. Let go of attachments, judgments and worries. There will be women who come who you don't even know when you put it out there. The circle itself has an energy field that will magnetize the exact right women. It's your job to simply bring awareness to the circle and hold down the stake in the ground so women know where to go.

Ask women to bring a friend or refer women to you. The sisterhood extends beyond your mind's eye. It is inclusive. It is diverse. Allow women to bring their friends who bring their friends. Create the space of non-judgment and openness and see who is curious to attend.

Write all names that come to you here:

_____

_____

_____

_____

_____

_____

_____

Making the Invitation

Circle is open! It is time to make the big announcement to the world...

Take Inspired Action!

1) Take a deep breath and go onto Facebook to write a post letting the world know that you are starting a circle.

Sample post for monthly circle gathering:

> Calling all goddesses! Are you looking to connect with the sisterhood where the conversations go deep and we support each other's brilliance? If so, come join us for a Full Moon Circle for ritual, movement, meditation, sharing and activation. [Link]

Sample post for 6 to 12-week circle experience:

> Ladies! I will be facilitating a [Virtual/Local] Sistership Circle [only can use our trademarked name if Certified] starting [next month] for up to 12 women. If you are looking for authentic connection with other leaders and aspiring leaders and an amazing structure to develop your leadership skills, this group is for you. If you are interested, private message me and I will give you more details and a formal invitation soon.

2) Send out at least 6 personal invitations via email, text or FB private message.

Sample message:

> Hi [name],
>
> I have felt the call to bring together some women for a sacred circle experience. It comes from a longing I have to go deeper with women and truly support each other's growth and expansion. You keep coming up for me. I feel a connection, like we are on the same page. If this is something that you've been wanting to call in too, I'd love to share with you what I am creating and see if you want to be part of it.
>
> Love,
> [your name]

Notes:

- ஃ Less is more.
- ஃ Get to the essence.
- ஃ Make the invitation personal (Why you want to connect with her personally.)
- ஃ Focus on what makes her special to you.
- ஃ Ask for a "date" to connect vs. a "relationship" right away.
- ஃ Your intention is to get interest. You are asking women to put their feet in the circle you are energetically standing in, and then they can choose to stay and take their seat if it feels right.
- ஃ You are setting up a *date* so you can both feel whether or not you want a *relationship*.

Integrate your Masculine and your Feminine

Masculine: Be Intentional and Deliberate.
Remember, you know what you want and you are taking inspired action. Go after it. Reach out.

Can you remember a time when you got really focused on a goal, laser focused, and made it happen? Nothing could stop you. You were so driven and committed.

Write that memory down. What happened? What did you feel? What can you draw from this experience?

_____

_____

_____

_____

Feminine: Co-Creative Leadership.
I am co-creating with the divine so I'm being sourced by something bigger than me. I am the channel, I am the circle. I am opening myself up to be sourced.

Can you remember a time when you trusted that you were supported by something bigger than yourself? Or when you didn't trust, but then after, everything worked out and you realized something bigger than you supported you?

Write that memory down. What happened? What did you feel? What can you draw from this experience?

_____

_____

_____

_____

Taking Payment

Because women believe that sisterhood should not be a commodity, many women think that circles should be free. I disagree. If you are putting time and effort into organizing a circle, expending energy holding the container and providing a valuable experience, then there should be an exchange of energy whether in the form of monetary payment or a barter.

Here's are three distinctions to make for yourself:

1) You are not selling sisterhood; you are providing an opportunity for women to learn valuable skills to create sisterhood in their lives.

2) You are providing a service to the community.

3) You are holding the space for a transformational experience, like a personal development workshop labeled as a circle.

This does not mean that you need to start charging for your circles right away. My suggestion is to find your comfort zone and threshold level and then gradually push that further out to where you want to be based on your income goals.

Example: let's say you want to make $500 a month. You are charging $15 per person. That means you need 33 women there to make your goal. Realistically, you are getting 15-20 women to attend so you want to gradually raise the cost of the circle to $20.

FREE
If you have never led a circle before, the key is in getting your feet wet and practicing to gain confidence, so a free circle may feel best for you. You may want to invite your friends and let them know you are leading for the first time and would like their feedback in exchange.

DONATION

If the circle is donation-based, make that clear on all of your marketing and give a suggested amount. Have a basket available at the door when women walk in. Chances are, they will not leave a donation until afterwards. When you are closing your circle, let women know that this was a donation based event. If you need to cover the cost of the venue, let the women know what that cost was and how much that is per person. If that is not the case, use the analogy of tipping your massage therapist when you get a massage or going to a nice restaurant. If you liked your experience, donate according to how much value you received.

FEE

Circle cost can range from $5 - 30. If you compare to a yoga class, the sweet spot is $11 - 20 per person. I prefer charging for circle because then I get a headcount of how many women are coming, and I also get women who are serious about circle.

If I charge, I always extend the invitation for 2 - 4 volunteers depending on the size of the gathering. This way I am providing an opportunity for women to attend who can't afford it.

You can create an early bird discount and a 2 for 1 special, which helps get women spreading the word and bringing a friend with them.

Set up an Eventbrite Event to take payment

If you are going to take payment, the best way is to set up an Eventbrite Event. They take a small fee, which you can select an option to have your guests pay. Then post the link on your Facebook event so people can register and reserve their seat in circle.

When you join our Facilitator Tribe or become Certified, we can post your event on our site for more exposure. All you need is a paypal link to receive direct payment.

Most Common Pitfalls + How To Avoid

Limited Belief #1: Women in my city are all flakes.

You can't possibly say that to me. I live in Southern California, the land of beach bums and non-committals. We are the stereotypical flakes.

But I don't subscribe to that belief. You attract what you put out there. I let women know the importance of being on time, registering on time, and showing up when they say they will show up. And I rarely have no-shows anymore.

The key is in being direct (in a kind, compassionate and loving way) and letting women know what to expect. Let them know the importance of showing up on time (because you are creating safe, sacred space). They will honor that when they understand.

Limited Belief #2: Women in my city don't pay for circle.

Many women subscribe to the belief that circle should be free, but it doesn't have to be. Know that you are providing a valuable service to your community. The more you own your value and worth, the easier the money will come and the less resistance you'll find from women.

Limited Belief #3: Women are too busy to commit to circle.

Everyone is busy, that's a fact for the modern day world. But we always make time for what we see is important and valuable. We commit to what we want to commit to. So if someone doesn't want to commit, it's just not for them ... right now. It may be for them at a later date. Trust that the right women will come together to gather. Trust that the timing is always right.

Marketing Made Easy

You don't need a website to hold circle! All you need is a Facebook event and the courage to announce it to your friends and larger community.

Set up a Facebook Event

Facebook is the best marketing tool out there because of the crowd-sourcing effect. When someone clicks that they are interested or going to an event, it shares it on their newsfeed so you can getting free marketing to their friends. They can also share it directly with their community and invite people.

If you are not on Facebook, I recommend creating your account simply so that you can use this tool to promote your circles.

Select Your Banner Image

Your banner image is the photo on the Facebook event and you want to select something that invoking the feeling you want women to get when they come to your circle. You can search for images on Google with terms like Goddess, Women's Circle, or the word that describes the theme of your circle.

Use This Marketing Copy (or create something similar)
AN INVITATION TO RISE, A CALL TO THE LIGHT

Our world is moving fast and we are struggling to stay connected with ourselves and one another.

Come and experience the magic that happens when women gather, open your heart, uncover your essence and get in touch with your greatness.

You are invited to reconnect with your wisdom, beauty, instincts, compassion and creativity to gain access to your deepest passions and desires.

If you are yearning connection, if you know that there is more of you that you would like to uncover, then this gathering is the place to be!

Walk your own path, find your own way! A world of celebration and possibility awaits.

If you have been looking for a place that provides safety to process, create, love, dance, laugh, cry or just be …

where your authentic self is always celebrated …

and you can open up to share desires, thoughts and feelings, I really hope you can make arrangements to be there.

Space is limited so save your seat today by registering at: LINK

Creating Your Own Marketing Copy
Go to Facebook.com/sistershipcircle and like our page. Then go to our events and look at any of the marketing copy that we use for our circles as an example of what to write.

When writing copy, you want to include the following: First line - A captivating and engaging first line such as a question

Credibility - What makes this circle special? What makes you special as a facilitator? If you are just starting off, then why a women's circle is important

Benefits - What will they walk away with? Why would someone want to come to circle? Use bullet points and make them enticing!

Testimonial - This is optional, but good to have if you've led circle before

Call to action - Ask them to register and save their seats

Step 5: Prepare
Prepare Your Circle Topic

*N*otice this is not the first thing I do. At the end of the day, it doesn't matter what topic you do, it matters who you are being and what your intention is. Now that you have committed, take some time to feel into a theme or topic that resonates with you.

We give circle outlines to you if you are a Facilitator Tribe member, taking away the worry and stress of designing a circle.

If you want to create your own, we also have a step-by-step process to use your intuition and creativity to Design Your Circle Outline (Below).

Time for Circle!

Your big day is right around the corner. In the next section, I'll tell you how to get ready so you feel prepared to lead your first circle … you've got this! Breathe … relax … believe in yourself. You are exactly where you are supposed to be. The exact right women will be there. There is no possible way you can fail … even if one woman shows up, it's perfect. Let go of any doubts, fears and worries. Let go of the pressure of doing it right or having it look a certain way. Remember, you are doing this circle FOR YOU, so as long as you get value, it's a win! And it will continue to improve with each circle you do.

Wisdom and confidence come from experience so let's seize this opportunity and get over the hurdle of doing your first one. It's always the hardest. And you are almost there!

Designing Your Circle Outline

Opening

- Decide how women will enter the space (cleansing with sage, in silence, etc)
- Opening Ceremony
- Grounding/Meditation
- Invocation
- Optional: music/chant/movement
- Connection exercise

Body of the Circle

- Introducing the topic
- Reading
- Short introduction
- Group share on topic

Break

- Movement/Music

Body of the Circle

- Diads or activity

Closing

- Sharing/Connecting Activity
- Closing ritual

Pre-Circle Checklist

Set up

- Chairs, pillows in a circle
- Altar or centerpiece of your choice in center of circle
- Candles and lighter by door
- Sage, rose water, or palo santo by door
- Potluck

Potluck

- Plates
- Silverware
- Cups
- Napkins
- Trash/recycling cans clearly marked

Handouts

- Commitments
- Schedule
- Circle roster
- Agreements
- Legal waivers
- Welcome
- Other _____
- Other _____

Altar/Centerpiece items

- Candles
- Lighter
- Colorful scarf
- Statues
- Rose petals (or other flower petals)

- ❍ Goddess deck cards
- ❍ Crystals
- ❍ Essential oils
- ❍ Other ____________________
- ❍ Other ____________________

Misc

- ❍ Blank paper
- ❍ Pens/pencils
- ❍ Timer
- ❍ Bell/chime
- ❍ Crystal bowls/singing bowls
- ❍ Music player and speakers
- ❍ Sage or palo santo
- ❍ Other ____________________
- ❍ Other ____________________

Resource & Book List

Communication Platforms

- Voxer
- Groupme
- Facebook Group

How to Lead Circle Meditations by Peta Bastian

"Calling In My Circle" download

"My Divine Feminine Leadership" download

"Opening to Receive Grounding Meditation" download

Our Favorite Books

Open Your Heart by Tanya Paluso on Amazon

The Millionth Circle by Jean Shinoda Bolen on Amazon

Urgent Message From Mother by Jean Shinoda Bolen on Amazon

Goddesses in Everywoman by Jean Shinoda Bolen on Amazon

4 Season in 4 Weeks on Amazon

Awakening Shakti by Sally Kempton on Amazon

Sacred Contracts by Caroline Myss on Amazon

The Heroine's Journey by Maureen Murdock on Amazon

The Book of SHE by Sara Avant Stover on Amazon

Wild Feminine by Tami Lynn Kent on Amazon

Red, Hot and Holy by Sera Beak on Amazon

Outrageous Openness by Tosha Silver on Amazon

Women Who Run with the Wolves by Clarissa Pinkola Estés on Amazon

Circle Round by Starhawk, Diane Baker and Anne Hall on Amazon

The Destiny of Women is the Destiny of the World by Guru Rattana on Amazon

A Woman's Worth by Marianne Williamson on Amazon

Circle of Stones by Judith Duerk on Amazon

Goddess Cards

Archetypes on Amazon

Gaia Oracle on Amazon

Goddesses on Amazon

Use the QR Code or go to https://sistershipcircle.com/startup-kit-links to access hyperlinks for the resources mentioned above.

Items to Purchase

Backjacks on Amazon

Indian chime cymbals on Amazon

Altar Centerpiece "Circle of Friends Candle Holder" on eBay

Lakshmi Statue on Amazon

Crystal Singing Bowl for Heart Chakra on Amazon

Sage Smudge Kit with Abalone Shell Stand Feather and White Sage on Amazon

Remo Buffalo drum

Indian Mandala Round Mat for Altar

Incense on Amazon

Candles on Amazon

Mandala Area Rug on Amazon

Mandala Towel on Amazon

Set SMART Goals

Leadership takes VISION and ACTION.

VISION:

WHY do you want to lead circle?

_____

_____

_____

_____

What do you personally want to receive from leading (and being in) circle?

_____

_____

_____

_____

What is your vision for women and circle in your city?

_____

_____

_____

_____

Create a roadmap to make it actionable so you can fulfill on your vision.

Goals should be SMART:

- ✿ Specific
- ✿ Measurable
- ✿ Attainable
- ✿ Relevant
- ✿ Timely

Start with CIRCLE:

How much money will you make?

6 month goal: _____

90 day goal: _____

This month: _____

How many circle gatherings will you host?

6 month goal: _____

90 day goal: _____

This month: _____

How many women will you serve?

6 month goal: _____

90 day goal: _____

This month: _____

Setting Up Your Sacred Space

*H*ow you set up the physical environment of the circle affects the sacredness. You can easily turn a white-walled boring room into a magical temple. Here are some ideas:

Entrance

Have music in the background as they cross the threshold into the circle space.

Either sage or anoint their third eye with a bindi or oil (if they so choose).

You can drape a beautiful fabric over the door.

Ask them to set an intention while they light a candle.

Altar

You can set up an altar in the middle of the circle however you wish. You can use flower petals, statues, candles, goddess cards, shells, or any other objects that have significance.

Here are some beautiful photos to inspire you:

Solstice Altar from HerSacredBody.com   GoddessRising.org

Seating
Best to have everyone sit on the floor with either pillows or backjacks.

If in chairs, have everyone be in a chair to create equality.

If there is a couch in the room, avoid using it. It creates too much casualness in the room.

Mood and Atmosphere
Candle lit creates a sacred atmosphere.

Use music at beginning to set the mood.

Your energy sets the tone. When you revere the space and go deep within yourself, the women will follow your lead.

Creating Your Agreements

When you craft your agreements, take into consideration the following items and decide how each one will be handled.

- Who is accountable for what
- Being on time and attending circle
- Keeping time during shares
- How to support a sister who is sharing emotions
- Confidentiality
- How to enter the space
- Refrain from gossip and other cattiness
- Refrain from feedback, cross talk, coaching

Full Moon Circles

The full moon is an excellent time to host your circle because it's a sacred time of the month when the moon illuminates and is in her fullest expression, a metaphor for women being in their full capacity and brilliance.

Suggested rituals and ideas for Full Moon Circles:

- Creativity and Self-Expression Themes
- Dance and move your body
- Release ceremony - the full moon is the begin the descent into the darkness
- Acknowledge the shadow of being in the bright light, "doing" energy (overwork ourselves to exhaustion, getting in our heads, too masculine)
- Reflect to and Celebrate one another - sharing, gratitude, sister support
- Share: what shadow is being illuminated by the full moon?

Check the moon dates here: http://www.moongiant.com/

Full Moon names date back to Native Americans, of what is now the northern and eastern United States. The tribes kept track of the seasons by giving distinctive names to each recurring full Moon. Their names were applied to the entire month in which each occurred. There was some variation in the Moon names, but in general, the same ones were current throughout the Algonquin tribes from New England to Lake Superior. European settlers followed that custom and created some of their own names. Since the lunar month is only 29 days long on the average, the full Moon dates shift from year to year. Here is the Farmers Almanac's list of the full Moon names.

Full Wolf Moon – January Amid the cold and deep snows of midwinter, the wolf packs howled hungrily outside Indian villages. Thus, the name for January's full Moon. Sometimes it was also referred to as the Old Moon, or the Moon After Yule. Some called it the Full Snow Moon, but most tribes applied that name to the next Moon.

Full Snow Moon – February Since the heaviest snow usually falls during this month, native tribes of the north and east most often called February's full Moon the Full Snow Moon. Some tribes also referred to this Moon as the Full Hunger Moon, since harsh weather conditions in their areas made hunting very difficult.

Full Worm Moon – March As the temperature begins to warm and the ground begins to thaw, earthworm casts appear, heralding the return of the robins. The more northern tribes knew this Moon as the Full Crow Moon, when the cawing of crows signaled the end of winter; or the Full Crust Moon, because the snow cover becomes crusted from thawing by day and freezing at night. The Full Sap Moon, marking the time of tapping maple trees, is another variation. To the settlers, it was also known as the Lenten Moon, and was considered to be the last full Moon of winter.

Full Pink Moon – April This name came from the herb moss pink, or wild ground phlox, which is one of the earliest widespread flowers of the spring. Other names for this month's celestial body include the Full Sprouting Grass Moon, the Egg Moon, and among coastal tribes the Full Fish Moon, because this was the time that the shad swam upstream to spawn.

Full Flower Moon – May In most areas, flowers are abundant everywhere during this time. Thus, the name of this Moon. Other names include the Full Corn Planting Moon, or the Milk Moon.

Full Strawberry Moon – June This name was universal to every Algonquin tribe. However, in Europe they called it the Rose Moon. Also because the relatively short season for harvesting strawberries comes each year during the month of June . . . so the full Moon that occurs during that month was christened for the strawberry!

The Full Buck Moon – July This is normally the month when the new antlers of buck deer push out of their foreheads in coatings of velvety fur. It was also often called the Full Thunder Moon, for the reason that thunderstorms are most frequent during this time. Another name for this month's Moon was the Full Hay Moon.

Full Sturgeon Moon – August The fishing tribes are given credit for the naming of this Moon, since sturgeon, a large fish of the Great Lakes and other major bodies of water, were most readily caught during this month. A few tribes knew it as the Full Red Moon because, as the Moon rises, it appears reddish through any sultry haze. It was also called the Green Corn Moon or Grain Moon.

Full Corn Moon or Full Harvest Moon – September This full moon's name is attributed to Native Americans because it marked when corn was supposed to be harvested. Most often, the September full moon is actually the Harvest Moon, which is the full Moon that occurs closest to the autumn equinox. In two years out of three, the Harvest Moon comes in September, but in some years it occurs in October. At the peak of harvest, farmers can work late into the night by the light of this Moon. Usually the full Moon rises an average of 50 minutes later each night, but for the few nights around the Harvest Moon, the Moon seems to rise at nearly the same time each night: just 25 to 30 minutes later across the U.S., and only 10 to 20 minutes later for much of Canada and Europe. Corn, pumpkins, squash, beans, and wild rice the chief Indian staples are now ready for gathering.

Full Hunter's Moon or Full Harvest Moon – October
This full Moon is often referred to as the Full Hunter's Moon, Blood Moon, or Sanguine Moon. Many moons ago, Native Americans named this bright moon for obvious reasons. The leaves are falling from trees, the deer are fattened, and it's time to begin storing up meat for the long winter ahead. Because the fields were traditionally reaped in late September or early October, hunters could easily see fox and other animals that come out to glean from the fallen grains. Probably because of the threat of winter looming close, the Hunter's Moon is generally accorded with special honor, historically serving as an important feast day in both Western Europe and among many Native American tribes.

Full Beaver Moon – November
This was the time to set beaver traps before the swamps froze, to ensure a supply of warm winter furs. Another interpretation suggests that the name Full Beaver Moon comes from the fact that the beavers are now actively preparing for winter. It is sometimes also referred to as the Frosty Moon.

The Full Cold Moon; or the Full Long Nights Moon – December
During this month the winter cold fastens its grip, and nights are at their longest and darkest. It is also sometimes called the Moon before Yule. The term Long Night Moon is a doubly appropriate name because the midwinter night is indeed long, and because the Moon is above the horizon for a long time. The midwinter full Moon has a high trajectory across the sky because it is opposite a low Sun.

Source: http://farmersalmanac.com/full-moon-names/

Other resource to check out: http://mysticmamma.org

Full Moon Gathering Outline

Entering the Space

Create sacred space: Have all women line up outside the space (even if in the hallway). Optional to sage/annoint each woman. When each woman comes to the front, give her a candle and ask her to hold the candle and focus on her intention for joining the circle. Tell her to enter the circle in silence, place her candle at altar and draw a goddess card. Then to sit in contemplation of her card in silence until circle begins.

Music playing in the background:

This is a great song, very inviting, ask them to just listen to the lyrics. It's called Ancient Mother: https://open.spotify.com/track/7jTt3OMjpJSu4SChJXQH74

Or this song called Bliss has no lyrics and is a good welcoming song into the space:

https://open.spotify.com/track/5rZmcTjrVjdr81mWso8lXY

Welcome

"Welcome to our [November Full Moon] Circle. First I want to thank you for whatever it took for you to get here tonight. Sometimes it isn't easy to show up but you did. Acknowledge yourself for that in this moment.

About this Full Moon

[Use Mysticmamma.com to pull a reading.]

Quick logistics: please take a bathroom break quietly when needed. If you need to leave early, please just sneak out, otherwise plan to stay here until 9pm.

First, we'll start with our opening meditation and invocation."

Opening Meditation

"Settle in your seat. Feel both feet on the floor. Close your eyes. As you take a few deep breaths, feel yourself going inward. Feel your body. Feel your heart. Feel your breath.

Notice any tension in the body. Send love to that area and ask it if it has something to tell you. Allow yourself to relax.

Allow yourself to be present in this body, in this room, in this circle.

Continue to be aware of your body as I read you the opening invocation."

Invocation

[Create your own invocation or become a Facilitator Tribe member to use ours.]

Bring Your Voice

Have everyone share their name and intention to bring their voice to the circle.

Hugs

"Now give everyone a hug hello!"

Agreements

To create safe space, we have three agreements.

First agreement: we hold what is shared here today in confidentiality. If you agree, please raise your hand and say YES.

Second agreement: we come to the circle open with no expectations. We each came here for a reason, so we are in trust of the medicine that circle offers each one of us. If you agree, please raise your hand and say YES.

Third agreement: we do not give one another feedback unless asked. Instead we beam one another at the end of a share. To beam, hold both your hands up like this (demonstrate) with palms facing the woman sharing. This is to honor and celebrate what she said so she feels seen, heard and valued. If you agree, please raise your hand and say YES.

Thank you everyone! Now we are going to move into the intention.

Intention for tonight: Full Moons are a time to bring conscious awareness to the past cycle: to illuminate the shadow to step fully into your light as well as to celebrate what's working, shifting and transforming. By sharing with our sisters, give ourselves permission to be our true selves with nothing to fix or change. We find our power by sharing our lives - both the messy and the pretty - with one another.

Take a few moments to think about the past moon cycle and the most challenging things you have faced. Is there any place that feels stuck, heavy or emotional? Is there something that you have started to work through? Is there something that you want to let go of, change or integrate?

Write in your journal or piece of paper your reflections.

Group Share

Share with the group for 3 minutes each what feels most alive. We invite you to share anything that you don't want to share; when we share our shame, it gets transformed and turns into light when our sisters hold us in unconditional love.

Know that we are holding a container of non-judgment, unconditional love and acceptance for all women exactly where you are at.

Full Moon Dance

https://soundcloud.com/deya-dova/sky-roarer

Chalice of Moon Wisdom Ritual

This ritual is best done to go outside under the full moon.

Fill a cup with well or spring water. Hold the cup up so that the light of the Full Moon shines upon the water it contains. Honor the Divine as Full Moon with the below invocation. Ask the Divine to energize the water and bless you with spiritual wisdom. Then drink of the water of the cup, meditate, and pay attention to any guidance you receive as you do this. Give thanks. Pour out any leftover water as an offering onto the land where you did the ritual.

Invocation:

> The moon is the symbol of the mother,
>
> and she watches over us day and night.
>
> She brings the changing tide, the shifting night,
>
> the flow that changes women's bodies,
>
> and the passion of lovers to their beloved.
>
> Her wisdom is great and all-knowing,
>
> and we honor her tonight.
>
> Keep your watchful eyes upon us, great mother,
>
> until the cycle returns once more,
>
> and bring us to the next full moon,
>
> in your love and light.

Celebration Ritual

Equally as challenging to share is our wins and celebrations. As women, we have been conditioned to dim our light so that we don't outshine others and make them feel less than. To end the evening, we are going to share one thing we celebrate about ourselves … it can be a quality that you embody or an accomplishment.

We will all stand in a circle and cheer on each woman as she steps into the circle and shares her win. Let her feel like she matters. Let her feel seen and valued!

Closing Ritual

Get in a circle, everyone turn to their left and place hands on the shoulders of the woman in front of them. Give the woman a massage. This is our closing ritual: a massage train. Just like we started with a stitch, we'll close with each woman sharing her name and one thing she has received from circle tonight that she will take home with her.

"I'm Tanya and I'm taking home connection with my creativity."

New Moon Circles

The new moon is also an excellent time to host your circle because it's a sacred time of the month when the moon is dark and at the end of a cycle. This is a potent time to plant dream seeds for the next cycle.

Suggested rituals and activities for New Moon Circles:

- Honor the darkness
- Honor the bleeding (see red tent)
- Tune into your psychic awareness and sensitivity
- Self-care - be gentle, look at your needs, nurturing space
- Journaling and reflecting on past cycle
- Honor the sacred pause
- Release ceremony for past cycle - water or fire
- Give and receive massage
- Plant dream seeds for next cycle: "I am creating …"

Seasonal Circles

Equinox

On the equinox, night and day are nearly the same length – 12 hours – all over the world. This is the reason it's called an "equinox", derived from Latin, meaning "equal night." However, in reality, equinoxes don't have exactly 12 hours of daylight.

The March equinox has long been celebrated as a time of rebirth in the Northern Hemisphere. Many cultures celebrate spring festivals and holidays around the March equinox, like Easter and Passover.

One of the most famous ancient Spring equinox celebrations was the Mayan sacrificial ritual by the main pyramid at Chichen Itza, Mexico. The main pyramid – also known as El Castillo – has bloody human sacrifices that used to take place here. The staircases are built at a carefully calculated angle which makes it look like an enormous snake of sunlight slithers down the stairs on the day of the equinox.

Vernal (Spring)

Spring is a time for rebirth, renewal, sewing new seeds, blossoming, and transformation. It also refers to love, hope, youth and growth.

Circle themes:
- ⚇ Health and Wellbeing
- ⚇ Starting New Projects and Brainstorming New Ideas
- ⚇ Blossoming/Coming Out of Shell
- ⚇ Maypole

Autumnal (Fall)

A season of transition, making final preparation for winter, harvesting and taking stock of all the abundance in our lives.

Circle themes:

- ✧ Abundance
- ✧ Gratitude
- ✧ Family
- ✧ Community
- ✧ Sisterhood and Celebration

Solstice

'Solstice' (Latin: 'solstitium') means 'sun-stopping'. The point on the horizon where the sun appears to rise and set, stops and reverses direction after this day. On the solstice, the sun does not rise precisely in the east, but rises to the north of east and sets to the north of west, meaning it's visible in the sky for a longer period of time.

Summer

The days are longer so there is no hiding, secrets or darkness. Summer is a time of light, joy, expression, vitality and action.

Circle Themes:

- ✧ Purification
- ✧ Fire Ceremony
- ✧ Passion
- ✧ Self-Expression

Winter

It's time to go inward for reflection, hibernation and reclusivity. Life is still and silent. Quiet the mind and still the soul. Gain purity and clarification.

Circle Themes:

- ✧ Reflection
- ✧ Self-Care
- ✧ Spirituality
- ✧ Self-Love

Wheel of the Year Circles

The **Wheel of the Year** is an annual cycle of seasonal festivals, observed by many modern Pagans. It consists of either four or eight festivals: either the solstices and equinoxes, known as the "quarter days", or the four midpoints between, known as the "cross quarter days"; syncretic traditions like Wicca often celebrate all eight festivals.

The festivals celebrated by differing sects of modern Paganism can vary considerably in name and date. Observing the cycle of the seasons has been important to many people, both ancient and modern, and many contemporary Pagan festivals are based to varying degrees on folk traditions.

Among Wiccans, the festivals are also referred to as *sabbats* /ˈsæbət/, with Gerald Gardner claiming this term was passed down from the Middle Ages, when the terminology for Jewish Shabbat was commingled with that of other *heretical* celebrations.

Source: https://en.wikipedia.org/wiki/Wheel_of_the_Year

- Midwinter (Yule) – Dec 20 - 23
- Imbolc – Feb 2
- Vernal Equinox (Ostara) – Mar 19 - 22
- Beltane - May 1
- Midsummer (Litha) - June 19 - 23
- Lammas/Lughnasadh – Aug 1
- Autumnal equinox (Mabon) – Sept 21 – 24
- Samhain – Nov 1

Beltane, and its counterpart Samhain, divide the year into its two primary seasons, winter (Dark Part) and summer (Light Part). As Samhain is about honoring Death, Beltane, its counter part, is about honoring Life. It is the time when the sun is fully released from his bondage of winter and able to rule over summer and life once again.

If this interests you, I invite you to do more research and create a circle to celebrate these holidays.

Red Tent Circles

The Red Tent, also known as the Moon Temple, comes from an ancient practice where women would gather in a tent during their period to rest together, usually during the new moon period. Red Tent Circles have the intention of creating safe, sacred space for women to honor their blood cycle and talk about all things related to being a woman: from fertility, infertility, pregnancy, birth, menstruation, menopause, dreams, motherhood, struggles, sistership, sexual identities and more.

If you are holding a red tent circle, consider the following:

Create a sacred space that is decorated in red and very comfortable with pillows, blankets, candles and a beautiful altar

Create a safe space that has agreements and permission for women to talk about anything on the entire spectrum from shame to celebration

Create a healing space for women to comfort each other, put healing hands on one another if someone so chooses, give massage and aromatherapy, take herbs and remedies, and lie down for rest

Create a nourishing space for women that includes food and drink to share

Create a connective space for women to feel the bonds of sisterhood through storytelling, singing, dancing and sharing

New Moon Gathering Outline

(please give credit to Sistership Circle by mentioning our name and website if using this curriculum)

Entering the Space

Create sacred space: Have all women line up outside the space (even if in the hallway). Optional to sage/annoint each woman. When each woman comes to the front, give her a candle and ask her to hold the candle and focus on her intention for joining the circle. Tell her to enter the circle in silence, place her candle at altar and draw a goddess card. Then to sit in contemplation of her card in silence until circle begins.

Music playing in the background:

This is a great song, very inviting, ask them to just listen to the lyrics. It's called Ancient Mother: https://open.spotify.com/track/7jTt3OMjpJSu4SChJXQH74

Or this song called Bliss has no lyrics and is a good welcoming song into the space:

https://open.spotify.com/track/5rZmcTjrVjdr81mWso8lXY

Welcome

"Welcome to our [November New Moon] Circle. First I want to thank you for whatever it took for you to get here tonight. Sometimes it isn't easy to show up but you did. Acknowledge yourself for that in this moment.

About this New Moon

Use Mysticmamma.com to pull a reading and share with the group the meaning of this new moon.

"Quick logistics: please take a bathroom break quietly when needed. If you need to leave early, please just sneak out, otherwise plan to stay here until 9pm.

First, we'll start with our opening meditation and invocation."

Opening Meditation

"Settle in your seat. Feel both feet on the floor. Close your eyes. As you take a few deep breaths, feel yourself going inward. Feel your body. Feel your heart. Feel your breath.

Notice any tension in the body. Send love to that area and ask it if it has something to tell you. Allow yourself to relax.

Allow yourself to be present in this body, in this room, in this circle.

Continue to be aware of your body as I read you the opening invocation."

Invocation

[Create your own invocation or become a Facilitator Tribe member to use ours.]

Bring Your Voice

Have everyone share their name and intention to bring their voice to the circle.

Hugs

"Now give everyone a hug hello!"

Agreements

To create safe space, we have three agreements.

First agreement: we hold what is shared here today in confidentiality. If you agree, please raise your hand and say YES.

Second agreement: we come to the circle open with no expectations. We each came here for a reason, so we are in trust of the medicine that circle offers each one of us. If you agree, please raise your hand and say YES.

Third agreement: we do not give one another feedback unless asked. Instead we beam one another at the end of a share. To beam, hold both your hands up like this (demonstrate) with palms facing the woman sharing. This is to honor and celebrate what she said so she feels seen, heard and valued. If you agree, please raise your hand and say YES.

Thank you everyone! Now we are going to move into the intention.

Intention for tonight: New Moons are a time to release the past cycle and plant dream seeds for the next cycle. It's a time to go inward and look at where we can be responsible for ourselves. Traditionally, women bleed with the new moon so it is the point of the month when women may be at their lowest energy and need to nurture themselves with self-care. It's the sacred pause. By sharing with our sisters, we give ourselves permission to be seen in our authenticity. We find our power by sharing our lives - both the messy and the pretty - with one another.

Take a few moments to think about the past moon cycle and the most challenging things you have faced. Is there any place that feels stuck, heavy or emotional? Is there something that you have started to work through? Is there something that you want to let go of, change or integrate?

Write in your journal or piece of paper your reflections.

Group Share

Share with the group for 3 minutes each what feels most alive. We invite you to share anything that you don't want to share; when we share our shame, it gets transformed and turns into light when our sisters hold us in unconditional love.

Know that we are holding a container of non-judgment, unconditional love and acceptance for all women exactly where you are at.

Goddess Bath Ritual (credit: Achintya and Sofiah Thom)

This is a release ritual where your sisters get to help you wash off the past cycle. Stand between two other sisters. As you state out loud what you want to release, the two women lovingly use their hands to wipe off energy from your body. They start from your head and go down to your feet. When finished (2-3 minutes each), give a bow of gratitude.

Sacred Pause

Lay down, get comfortable, allow yourself to just be in the sacred pause during this song: https://soundcloud.com/eub-motega-8/native-american-indian-spirit (play for 5-6 minutes)

Or

https://soundcloud.com/imaginedherbalflows/ihf-fade

Plant Dream Seeds Ritual

What are you planting for the next cycle? What do you want to call in?

In the middle of the circle, state your intention: "I am _____."

Everyone says "And so it is!" in unison response.

Closing Ritual

Get in a circle, everyone turn to their left and place hands on the shoulders of the woman in front of them. Give the woman a massage. This is our closing ritual: a massage train. Just like we started with a stitch, we'll close with each woman sharing her name and one thing she has received from circle tonight that she will take home with her.

"I'm Tanya and I'm taking home connection with my creativity."

Ask her to sit in silence to honor the space.

Music at Your Circle

Music Playlists

Sistership Circle Soundcloud

Sistership Circle Spotify

Sistership Circle Podcast

Sistership Circle Playlist

Michelle Rowland's Women's Circle Playlist

Circle of Women Album

Goddess Chants

Women's Circle Youtube Playlist

Favorite Artists

Marya Stark

Scarlet Crow

Deya Dova

Peia

Peruquois

Brooke Medicine Eagle

Sasha Butterfly

Beautiful Chorus

Rising Appalachia

Jennifer Berezan

Shylah Ray Sunshine

Tenru

Use the QR Code or go to https://sistershipcircle.com/startup-kit-links to access hyperlinks for the artists mentioned above.

When to use music

- ⚛ When women are entering the space
- ⚛ During any journaling exercises
- ⚛ During a dance break
- ⚛ At the end to leave on a positive, upbeat note

Dance Break

If you are embarrassed or shy about dancing, or perhaps are afraid if women will want to dance or not, use this activity called Follow The Leader. Everyone gets in a circle and you start. You make up easy dance moves like Staying Alive index pointing up and down and everyone follows your lead. Then you point at the next woman and she makes up the next dance moves and when she's had enough she selects the next person and so on until the end of the song.

Some pop songs we've used that are upbeat:

Taylor Swift - Shake it Off

Black Eyed Peas - Let's Get This Party Started

Maklemore - Can't Hold Us

Natasha Beddingford - Unwritten

Katy Perry - Roar

Essential Oils for Circle

- ᯤ Frankincense: The Oil of Truth
- ᯤ Lavender: The Oil of Communication
- ᯤ Bergamot: The Oil of Self Acceptance
- ᯤ Geranium: The Oil of Love & Trust.

- ᯤ Wild Orange: The Oil of Abundance
- ᯤ Clary Sage: The Oil of Clarity & Vision
- ᯤ Myrrh: The Oil of Mother Earth
- ᯤ Sandalwood: The Oil of Sacred Devotion

Where to purchase

While many women sell oils from well known network marketing companies like Young Living and Doterra, these are mass farmed and the quality could be jeopardized. There are many small sustainable companies to research locally in your part of the world.

It's important to note the difference between farmed and wildcrafted and to understand which plants are "endangered."

Sandalwood, Frankincense and Rosewood are all on the endangered list and should be bought from sustainable farmers instead of wildcrafted.

You can check this list: https://www.iucnredlist.org/

Some of my favorite oils are made by Scent Priestess Diana Dubrow at https://www.emeraldtemple.com/store

How to anoint

Step 1: First add essential oils to a base carrier like Jojoba oil. You can create custom blends this way.

Step 2: Add a few drops to your hands and rub your hands together. Smell the oil deeply.

Step 3: Pass your hands above your auric field.

Step 4: Place your hands on a part of your body that you feel called to anoint. This could be any chakra point or the feet.

Post Circle
Playsheets

Post-Circle Inventory Evaluation

Checking in with yourself

How is your energy level on a scale of 1 to 10 after circle?

Celebrating yourself

What worked?

What were your favorite frames?

What positive things were said about circle by the women?

What did you love about the circle?

What did you love about your leadership?

What were you proud of?

Improving for next time

What didn't work?

Were all the agreements upheld?

Was anything off?

Was anyone complaining about anything?

Follow up items

Was anyone crying or emotional?

Did anyone leave withdrawn or upset?

Were any withholds expressed that may have been misinterpreted?

Did anyone fight or have an exchange?

Was anyone absent or late? Did you address it?

** REMEMBER: circle is a mirror of YOU. Avoid the temptation to blame others. You claim your power back when you take full responsibility for everything that happens in circle. Ask yourself: *what is this conflict or outward challenge reminding me of within myself or in my own life? What healing is the universe inviting me to do in myself by showing me this mirror in front of me?*

Post-Circle Integration

How will you take care of yourself?

- Bubble bath
- Epsom Salt bath
- Shower
- A gentle walk
- Meditation
- Journaling

Who will you call to hold space for you and help you clear if circle was heavy?

- Coach
- Buddy
- Colleague
- Therapist

Forms
and
Handouts

Photo, Video and Audio Release Form

Date: _____

The undersigned enters into the following agreement ("Agreement") with _____ ("Producer"). I have been informed that Producer is capturing footage and that my name, likeness, image, voice, appearance and/or performance is being recorded and made part of the recording in which I appear ("Product").

1. I grant Producer and its designees the right to use the Product in any format, now known or later developed. I grant, without limitation, the right to edit, mix or duplicate and use or re-use Product in whole or in parts as Producer may elect. Producer or its designees have complete ownership of the Product, including copyright interests.

2. I grant Producer and its designees the right to broadcast, exhibit, market and otherwise distribute the Product, in whole or in parts, and alone or with other products, for any purpose Producer or its designees determine. This grant includes the right to use Product for promoting or publicizing.

3. I have the right to enter into Agreement and am not restricted by commitments to third parties.

4. Producer has no financial commitment or obligations to me as a result of Agreement.

5. In consideration of all the above, I hereby acknowledge receipt of reasonable and fair consideration from Producer. I have read, understand and agree to all of the above and that the rights granted Producer herein are perpetual and worldwide:

_____   _____
Name   Signature

General Liability Release Agreement

Date: _____

Not Therapy: _____ ("Participant") understands that circle is not to be used as a substitute for professional advice by legal, mental, medical or other qualified professionals and will seek independent professional guidance for such matters. If Participant is currently under the care of a mental health professional, _____ ("Producer") will recommend that Participant inform the mental health care provider.

Limited Liability: Except as expressly provided in this agreement, Producer makes no guarantees or warranties, express or implied. In no event will Producer be liable to the Participant for consequential or special damages. Notwithstanding any damages that the Participant may incur, Producer's entire liability under this agreement, and the Participant's exclusive remedy, will be limited to the amount paid by the Participant to Producer under this agreement for all services rendered up until the program end date.

This is the entire agreement of the parties, and reflects a complete understanding of the parties with respect to the subject matter. This agreement supersedes all prior written and oral representations.

If a dispute arises out of this agreement that cannot be resolved by mutual consent, the Participant and Producer agree to attempt to mediate in good faith for up to (certain amount of time such as 30 days) after notice given. If the dispute is not resolved, and in the event of legal action, the prevailing party shall be entitled to recover attorney's fees and court costs from the other party.

Applicable Law: This contract shall be governed by the laws of the State of CA in San Diego County and any applicable Federal Law.

_____   _____
Name   Signature

Sign In Sheet

Name	Email	Phone

Feedback Form

What is your facilitator doing that works?

_____

_____

_____

What is your facilitator doing that doesn't work?

_____

_____

_____

What do you like the most about the circle?

_____

_____

_____

What do you dislike about the circle?

_____

_____

_____

Do you have any withholds (any uncommunicated charge around another woman in the circle or the group)?

_____

_____

_____

_____

_____

Testimonial Form

Your testimonial is the #1 way you can thank us for creating this sacred space. Your referrals are the second. Please take a moment to write a sincere testimonial that we can feature on our website. Include your name, city and website.

Name: _____

City: _____ Website: _____

_____

_____

_____

_____

_____

_____

_____

_____

_____

_____

_____

_____

_____

_____

_____

_____

_____

_____

Next Steps

Looking for more training and development?

Whether you are looking for more training to …

- ꩜ build confidence to start your first circle,
- ꩜ increase your sense of self-worth to charge for your circles,
- ꩜ or build a business running circles and retreats …

Sistership Circle is here to support you!

Our programs are focused on giving you the confidence, clarity and courage to step into your feminine leadership in your family, community and the world at large.

Being a facilitator is an opportunity to heal, connect and integrate yourself first, so you can be the model for others to follow.

We are calling to join our feminine leadership movement where we all join hands in sisterhood across the planet.

Here are the ways we can support you:

Join a Local or Virtual Circle
Sit in one of our many circles led by certified facilitators around the world at
https://sistershipcircle.com/events/

The Art of Leading Circle
Learn how to fill, lead and grow your circle with this 44-module video course at
https://sistershipcircle.com/art-of-leading-womens-circle

Become a Sistership Circle Facilitator

Learn more about our certification and licensing path at http://sistershipcircle.com/become-a-facilitator

How to Lead Circle

Take the 12-week intense Level 1 Certification where you get to practice your facilitation and get coaching support to start your first circle by the end of the program at https://sistershipcircle.com/how-to-lead-circle/

About the Author

Tanya Lynn is a "strategic activator" — gifted at coaching women to soar to new heights by putting together a plan that maximizes their talents and strengths and taking bold, courageous actions to fulfill on their intentions.

Tanya is the visionary CEO behind the international organization, Sistership Circle, a worldwide sisterhood movement empowering women to step into their true beauty, brilliance and boldness as feminine leaders. She started training facilitators to use her proven 12-week Circle Program based on her bestselling book "Open Your Heart: How to be a New Generation Feminine Leader." She is also the author of "How to Lead Circle."

She is a respected leader in the industry from clients and colleagues alike because she's the real deal, living and breathing her work.

She believes that the new model of feminine leadership is not about hierarchies of power but about circles of collaboration. For us to become true leaders, we must embrace our sisters as our allies and give one another permission to shine.

Learn more about Tanya here.

Made in the USA
Monee, IL
26 October 2021